Keys Desert Queen Ranch:
A Visual & Historical Tour

JOSHUA TREE
NATIONAL PARK

Enjoy the tour.
Thomas Crochetiere

Books by Thomas Crochetiere:

The JTNP series;

The History of Joshua Tree National Park –
History [2019; Forth Edition, 6/2022]

Keys Desert Queen Ranch: A Visual & Historical Tour –
History [2020]

The Trail Guide to Joshua Tree National Park –
Hiking – History [2022]

Also by Thomas Crochetiere;

Remembering my Miss Vicki –
a Biography [2011]

Our Life Well-Lived –
a Memoir [2012]

America's National Parks At a Glance –
Travel [2016]

Gateway to the Morongo Basin –
History [2021]

A Treasure of Fine Words –
Literature / Book of Quotations [2022]

Cover and back ranch photos by Thomas Crochetiere

Back photo of Thomas by Kevin Wong –
JTNPA/Desert Institute

Keys Desert Queen Ranch:
A Visual & Historical Tour

JOSHUA TREE
NATIONAL PARK

By
Thomas Crochetiere

Contact the author at:
tcrochetiere@outlook.com

ISBN: 978-1-63901-928-1

Printed in the United States of America

Proofread by Jacqueline Guevara

Published in cooperation with:
JOSHUA TREE NATIONAL PARK ASSOCIATION
74485 National Park Drive
Twentynine Palms, California 92277
www.joshuatree.org

(also available in eBook format)

Table of Contents

Acknowledgments   vi

Introduction   vii

Ranch Map   0

Joshua Tree National Park   1

The Camp and Mill Site   5

Bill and Frances Keys   10

Desert Queen School   21

The Ranch and the NPS   23

The Ranch Tour   28

From Cabin to Ranch House   70

The Dams Protecting the Ranch   76

The Ranch under the Stars   79

The Ranch in the Snow   82

The 1976 Tour Guide   84

Homesteads   86

Mines and Mills   87

About the Author   88

Acknowledgments

Research material from the Joshua Tree National Park Library; including books, reports, studies, and reference materials were used to help create this visual and historical tour of Bill and Frances Keys Desert Queen Ranch. Information found on NPS.gov was also used. I would like to credit and thank the following resources for their contributions to the writing of this book. Writings of Willis Keys, Art Kidwell, Jeff Ohlfs, and David Glasgow were used to verify and confirm some of the ranch and park history.

I would like to give thanks to Jacqueline Guevara, Executive Director for JTNPA, Jason Theuer, Cultural Resource Branch Chief for JTNP, Cane West, Ph.D., Park Ranger – Interpretation Division for JTNP, Dave Larson, Park Ranger - Interpretation Division for JTNP, and to Sandra Crochetiere (my wife) for their contributions to my writings.

My thanks also go out to photographer Marjorie Trandem, the NPS, JTNPA, and Action 29 Palms for use of their photos and murals to help tell the story of the Keys Desert Queen Ranch tour.

We will be forever grateful to the Keys family and heirs for their continued support as we share the family history and keeping the memories alive though the ranch tours and this and every publication about Keys Desert Queen Ranch.

Unless otherwise indicated, photos throughout this book were taken by Thomas and Sandra Crochetiere.

Introduction

Keys Desert Queen Ranch is located in a remote, rocky canyon of Joshua Tree National Park. The area was first occupied by seasonal American Indians. Later cattlemen arrived to graze and water their cattle while establishing a camp there. Once gold was discovered, the area was transformed into a mill site. It was not until Bill Keys moved there when he began building his ranch, the Desert Queen Ranch.

Bill and Frances Keys spent over 44 years working together to make a life and raise a family in this secluded location. Living nearly 60 miles away from the nearest town meant they would have to live without the common comfort's others took for granted.

The guided tour of the ranch includes the colorful story of the Keys family. The ranch house, storehouse, schoolhouses, machine shop, out-buildings, a corral, windmill and wells, stamp-mill, and arrastra can be seen there today. The orchard and irrigation system are still visible; and the grounds are full of the cars, trucks, mining equipment, farm equipment, and spare parts that are a part of the Desert Queen Ranch story.

Every effort was made to verify the accuracy of the ranch history; however, the author found some conflicting statements as to the exact year some of the following history occurred. Any corrections or suggested additions are welcome.

NO ONE is allowed on ranch property without being escorted by a park ranger or authorized park staff.

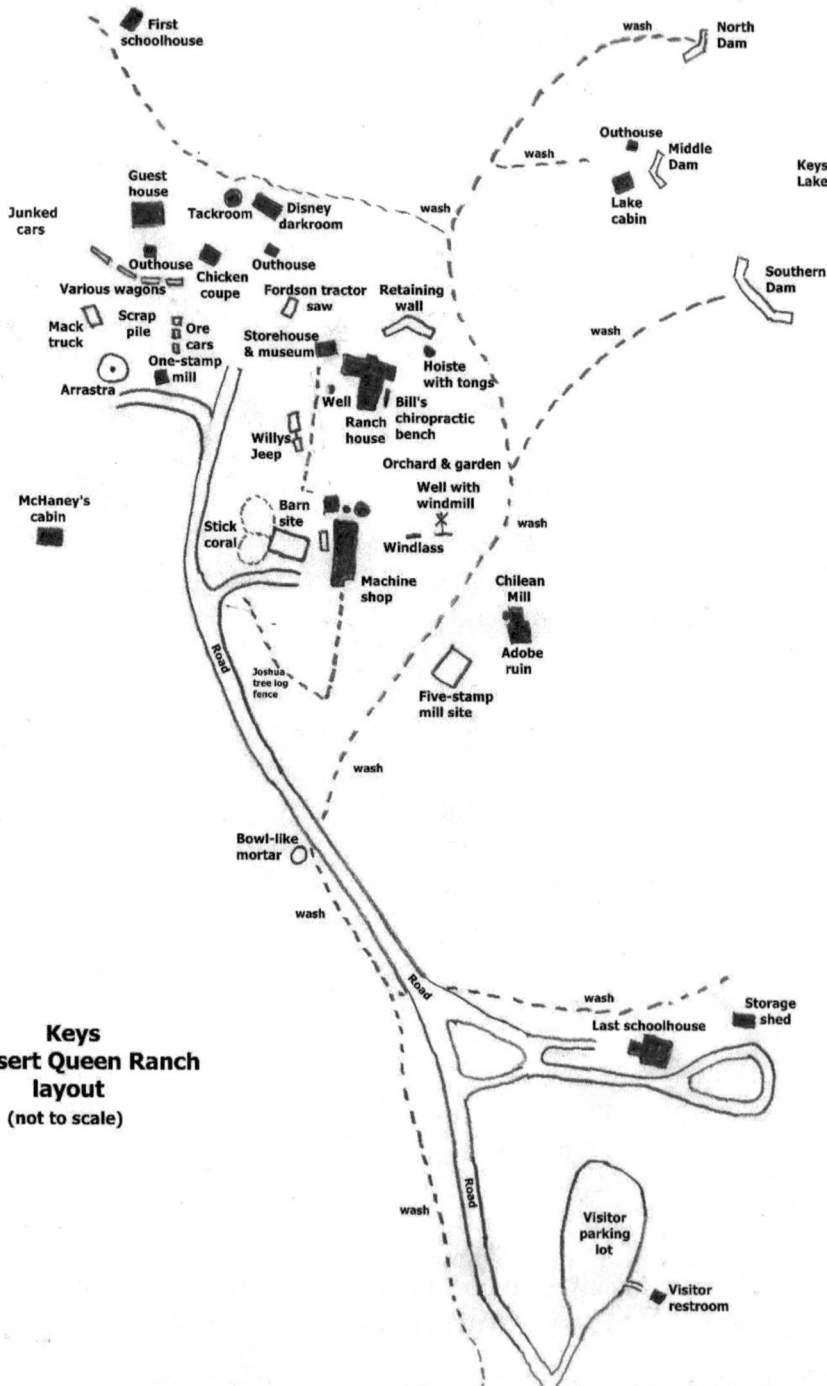

**Keys
Desert Queen Ranch
layout**
(not to scale)

First schoolhouse

North Dam

wash

Outhouse

Middle Dam

Keys Lake

wash

Lake cabin

Junked cars

Guest house

Tackroom

Disney darkroom

wash

Southern Dam

Outhouse

Chicken coupe

Outhouse

Various wagons

Fordson tractor saw

Retaining wall

wash

Mack truck

Scrap pile

Ore cars

Storehouse & museum

Hoiste with tongs

One-stamp mill

Well

Bill's chiropractic bench

Arrastra

Willys Jeep

Ranch house

Orchard & garden

McHaney's cabin

Stick coral

Barn site

Well with windmill

wash

Windlass

Machine shop

Chilean Mill

Joshua tree log fence

Adobe ruin

Five-stamp mill site

wash

Bowl-like mortar

wash

Road

wash

Last schoolhouse

Storage shed

Road

wash

Visitor parking lot

Visitor restroom

0

Joshua Tree National Park

Joshua Tree National Park preserves a world-renowned population of Joshua trees. These Joshua tree forests intermingle with massive boulder formations of 85-million-year-old monzogranite. Other rock formations within the park contain 1.4 to 1.7-billion-year-old Pinto Gneiss and 2 to 3-million-year-old black basalt.

There are more than one species of Joshua tree. Yucca brevifolia (western Joshua tree) is found in Joshua Tree National Park while Yucca jaegeriana (eastern Joshua tree) is found in the Mojave National Preserve. Yucca brevifolia's trunk is typically longer and looks more like a stereotypical tree where the Yucca jaegeriana is more bush like and tends to be smaller, with branches radiating close to the ground. Yucca brevifolia is the largest of the yuccas and both are members of the Agave family.

Joshua trees (and most other yuccas) rely on the female Yucca Moth for pollination. The moth lays her eggs in the flower ovary, and when the larvae hatch, they feed on the yucca seeds. The Yucca brevifolia and Yucca jaegeriana rely on separate Yucca Moth species for pollination. The flowers of each kind of Joshua tree have distinct shapes that fit the egg-laying organ of their respective moth. The Joshua tree and Yucca Moth are dependent upon each other in order to reproduce. Although older Joshua trees (which really aren't trees) can sprout new plants from their roots, only the seeds produced in pollinated flowers can scatter far enough to establish a new stand.

Joshua Tree National Park is a vast protected area in Southern California where two distinct desert ecosystems, the Mojave and the Colorado, come together. Evidence of ancestral peoples can be found as well as the history of cattle grazing, mining, and early pioneers.

On August 10, 1936, Joshua Tree National Monument (JTNM) was established by Presidential Proclamation under the Antiquities Act of 1906. The creation of Joshua Tree National Monument was signed into law by President Franklin D. Roosevelt. The new monument protected approximately 825,340 acres, and is managed by the National Park Service (NPS).

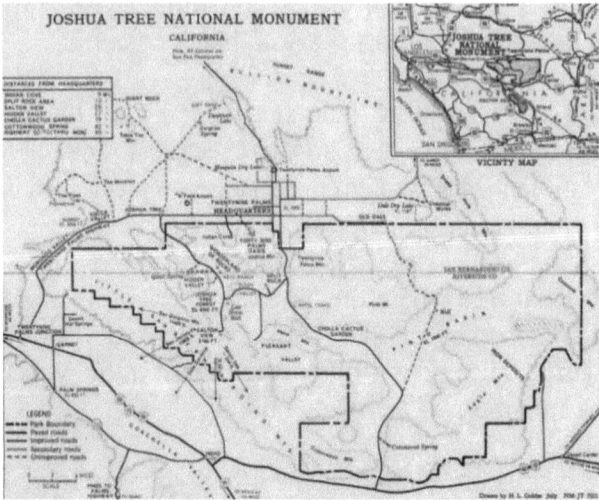

1936 boundary map of Joshua Tree National Monument; drawn by H.L. Golder

In 1950, Congress reduced the size of JTNM by 289,500 acres. The areas eliminated from the park were those in which it was thought that mining and grazing in commercial quantities could be developed.

Under the California Desert Protection Act of 1994, Joshua Tree National Monument was abolished and its lands incorporated into Joshua Tree National Park (JTNP). Under this act, the new national park was enlarged. The act was passed by the United States Congress on October 8, 1994 and signed into law by President Bill Clinton, taking effect on October 31, 1994. This Act also established Death Valley National Park, the Mojave National Preserve, and 69 wilderness areas in the California Desert.

Joshua Tree National Park is open year-round. There are few facilities within the parks nearly 800,000 acres, making Joshua Tree a true desert wilderness. There is no electricity or drinking water throughout the majority of Joshua Tree National Park. Vault toilets are located in all campgrounds and picnic areas, and most trailheads and parking lots. There are no places to get food, gas, lodging, or other services within the park. **Drinking water filling stations are located at** the Oasis of Mara parking lot, Cottonwood Visitor Center, the West Entrance Station, Indian Cove Ranger Station, and Black Rock Nature Center.

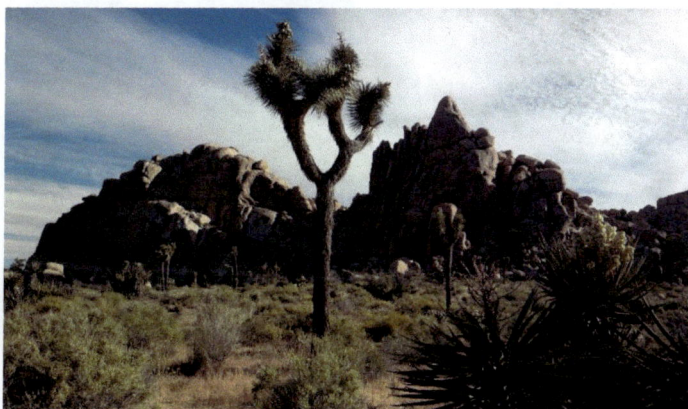

The park's physical address is 74485 National Park Drive Twentynine Palms, CA 92277-3597. The website is https://www.nps.gov/jotr. Call **1-760-367-5500** for more information or email at jotr_info@nps.gov.

In the event of an emergency and if you are in a location with cell phone service, **dial 911 or call 1-909-383-5651**. Do not depend on your cell phone in an emergency as cell coverage is very limited inside the park! **Emergency phones** are located at the ranger station in Indian Cove, in the parking lot at Intersection Rock (next to Hidden Valley Campground and across from the entrance to Hidden Valley picnic area), and at the Cottonwood Visitor Center.

Located in the heart of Joshua Tree National Park, Keys Desert Queen Ranch is a well-preserved homestead (read more about homesteads on page 86). The ranch is located at the southernmost edge of the Mojave Desert, in an area of the park known as the Wonderland of Rocks. It is closed to public access and is only accessible via a 90-minute guided tour. Bill Keys and the Desert Queen Ranch are a cornerstone of Joshua Tree National Park.

Keys Desert Queen Ranch; a preservation of the past

The Camp and Mill Site

Archeological evidence of the area was found in the southern half (Colorado Desert portion; part of the larger Sonoran Desert) of present-day Joshua Tree National Park. Projectile points and milling tools found there date back 4 to 8 thousand years ago. These artifacts were left behind from the period of the Pinto Culture.

Following the Pinto Culture, the Serrano Indians (Maara'yam People) inhabited the northern half (Mojave Desert portion; also known as the high desert) of present-day Joshua Tree National Park. The Cahuilla Indians (Kawiya People) inhabited the southern half (also known as the low desert). The Chemehuevi Indians (Nuwu People) and Mohave Indians (Macave People) from the Colorado River region also traveled throughout the area. Though mostly seasonal, the Serrano and later Chemehuevi settled at the Oasis of Mara in present-day Twentynine Palms, CA. Many of these Indians would frequent springs and other known water sources within present-day Joshua Tree National Park, including along the present-day Barker Dam trail and a spring at present-day Keys Desert Queen Ranch.

Barker Dam Petroglyphs

William Lafayette "Bill" McHaney (born on March 25, 1859) is believed to be the first permanent non-native to settle in the Twentynine Palms area, arriving in 1879. He lived in a small shack at the Oasis of Mara. Prior to McHaney, the oasis was settled by American Indians and also used by non-native people as a stopover point where prospectors, cattleman, and travelers could rest and get water before moving on.

In the early 1880s, Bill McHaney and his brother James "Jim" McHaney grazed Texas Longhorn cattle in the Hidden Valley area of present-day Joshua Tree National Park. Around 1888, they started development on a camp there. The location was ideal for ranching because of its access to year-round water and grazing, as well as its proximity to mining locations for gold prospecting. At first, they built two adobe cabins; one was used as a bunkhouse and the other as a cookhouse. In 1894 they built an adobe barn. Their camp came to be known as the "McHaney Camp."

After acquiring ownership of the Desert Queen Mine in 1894, Bill and Jim McHaney received financing from a bank in Los Angeles, CA to purchase and have installed a five-stamp mill from Baker Ironworks of Los Angeles at the McHaney Camp in 1895 (read more about stamp mills on page 64). Baker Ironworks ran the Desert Queen Mine and new mill until the mill was paid for. After it was paid off, the McHaney brothers took over the mine and mill site (read more about mines and mills on page 87).

The initial gold found at the Desert Queen Mine was extremely rich, but the wealth was spent as soon as it was produced. With the high costs of mining and milling in the desert, the McHaneys quickly exhausted all available funds. To help cover costs, the brothers took out a new loan from a bank in San Bernardino, CA.

The Desert Queen Mine was involved in much litigation during the last few months of 1895. The bank took possession of the mine and mill site which were then sold to W.M. MacMillen of Denver, CO. Bill McHaney remained in the area but Jim McHaney left.

In 1896, the Desert Queen Mine and mill site were again sold, this time to C.M. Thompson of Pasadena, CA, and financed by Zambro Bank in San Bernardino. Under supervision of S. F. Zambro, the mine and mill site were managed for a time by Carrie McHaney Harrington (sister to Bill and Jim).

The Desert Queen Mine and Mill site were sold to San Bernardino banker S.F. Zambro in 1902. Buying the mine as an investment, Zambro did not do much work at the site.

In 1907, Desert Queen Mine and Mill site were sold to William Morgan of Pasadena. Morgan, a man in his 80s, immediately began to invest in the sites, making many additions and improvements.

Desert Queen Mine; NPS photo

In 1908, William Morgan had a well dug and windmill installed along the present-day Wall Street Mill Trail to produce water for the nearby Desert Queen Mine. He called this the Desert Queen Well.

William "Bill" Keys arrived in the area in 1910, at the age of 30. At first, he worked as a cowboy and lived in the Surprise Spring area north of the present-day town of Joshua Tree, CA. Bill Keys then began work as a muleskinner for the Desert Queen Mine and started living at the McHaney Camp and mill site. Keys quickly became friends with Bill McHaney, who frequented the camp. Bill Keys began doing assessment work for William Morgan at the Desert Queen Mine and remained living at the mill site.

In 1913, Bill Keys started to build a permanent cabin to live in while staying at the Desert Queen Mill site. William Morgan died in 1915 owing Bill back wages. Bill filed against the estate for the money owed to him. Bill McHaney abandoned any claim of the McHaney Camp and Bill Keys filed a homestead on it, including the mill site. Keys began to construct his ranch, calling it the "Desert Queen Ranch."

After the death of William Morgan, Morgan's attorney deeded the Desert Queen Mine to Bill Keys in lieu of back wages owed to Keys in 1917. Keys then became the new owner of the Desert Queen Mine, its cabins, and its mining equipment. The Desert Queen Mine was one of the most productive mines in the area.

At the age of 39, Bill Keys married Frances May Lawton of Pasadena on October 8, 1918 and brought her to Desert Queen Ranch; she was 31 (some accounts list her middle name spelled Mae). Bill soon began to enlarge the cabin while they started their family. He and Frances made a life and raised their children in this remote desert location. Through their hard work, they built one of the largest, most self-sustaining ranches of its kind in the area.

Bill and Frances Keys

Life in the desert presented many challenges. Summers were extreme and there would be several years with little or no rainfall. Crops would fail and water wells ran dry. The work was hard and neighbors far away. Few homesteaders met the challenge. Many farms and small homesteads were abandoned, leaving behind the tiny cabins which still litter the desert in places today. Food and supplies were difficult to come by. The closest town of Banning, CA was nearly 60 miles away. They had to travel on a rough, deeply rutted dirt road to get there. "One family that not only survived but thrived in the desert was that of Bill and Frances Keys."

Bill Keys was born on September 27, 1879 in Nebraska. His name at birth was George Barth. He had 10 brothers and sisters. After a dispute with his father, he left home at the age of 15 in 1894. In 1898, for unknown reasons, he changed his name to William Franklin Key.

In 1917, Bill Key added "s" to his last name due to mail confusion with the Kee family living nearby. Although spelled differently, both names were pronounced the same.

Over the years, Bill obtained a vast amount of knowledge of just about everything he would need to survive, raise a family, and prosper. Through Bill's many experiences, he learned everything from nature, to the stars and universe, to animals, farming, and mineralogy. He knew most of the names of the rocks in the area and what minerals were in them by examining them. Just by looking at the formations around, he knew what areas were good for prospecting. Bill was also an accomplished blacksmith and could do just about anything with scrap metal.

Bill spent long hours tending to livestock such as mules, burros, horses, cattle, goats, chickens, milk cows, and whatever they would need to survive. He had an amazing orchard and garden as well as crop fields. Bill had up to 30 mines at one time and worked each of them until they had nothing more to give. Bill ran one or more mills, mostly processing ore for other mines, charging them by the ton.

Bill also owned many homestead sites. He sold some, even holding the note on them. If needed, he foreclosed on them if the buyer stopped making payments.

When other miners would give up and walk away from their claims, Bill would file a new claim on them and either work the mine or just repurpose anything they may have left behind. Bill often sold such items to new or existing miners who were in need. He would sell what mines he no longer wanted or needed or he would lease a mine to anyone who wanted to give a try to find their riches.

Bill Keys; NPS photo

Frances May Lawton was born on September 24, 1887 in Ohio. She had 3 brothers and 3 sisters. Frances worked in Los Angeles for several years as a stenographer and also for Western Union as a telegrapher, which is where she is believed to have met Bill (conflicting stories have been shared as to how they actually met).

After her marriage to Bill Keys, Frances worked very hard and tried to keep everything clean. She did all the housework, washed the clothes by hand, and did the canning during canning season. Frances was an excellent cook, cooking from memory and did not rely on recipes. If beef was not available, she would use chicken, domestic rabbit, cottontail, or jackrabbits. She always made sure there was plenty to eat for breakfast and dinner. Frances was very creative and knew how to make things last. She knew how to sew and taught her kids the same. Frances tended to the garden and ran the chicken and rabbit pens. She even assisted with the mining. Although not having formal training, she was also an informative teacher.

Frances Keys gave birth to their first son, William Jr. in September 1919. He would die just 5 days later. On January 5, 1921, their second child Willis was born. On January 3, 1923, Bill and Frances' third child Virginia was born. In August 1924, their fourth child was born; David would also die just 5 days after his birth. On August 31, 1926, Ellsworth, their fifth child was born. On October 18, 1928, Patricia their sixth child was born; and on October 3, 1931, their seventh and last child, Phyllis was born. Their deceased children were buried in a family cemetery Bill erected away from their ranch.

Bill with Willis, Virginia, Ellsworth, and Patricia;
NPS photo

Not long after his arrival to the area, Bill Keys became friends with an old-time miner named Johnny Lang. On January 25, 1926, Johnny tacked a note on his shack saying to the effect "Gone for grub. Be back soon." He died along the trail next to what is now known as Keys View Road. His mummified body was found two months later on March 25th by Bill Keys along with Jeff Peeden and Frank Kiler. A grave was dug and he was buried on the spot.

Photo of Bill Keys with Jeff Peeden taken by Frank Kiler; NPS photo

Starting in 1927, famed lawyer and author Erle Stanley Gardner visited the area of present-day Joshua Tree National Park and befriended Bill Keys. Gardner would often return for a visit with Bill and his family at their Desert Queen Ranch.

Bill Keys purchased the nearby Wall Street Mill in 1930 from local miner Oran Booth and his partner Earle McInnis, and began to spend a lot of his time there making improvements to the site. He acquired the old two-stamp mill at Pinyon Well from Fred Vaile of the New Eldorado Mining Company and had it placed next to a wash near an old arrastra along the road south of the Wall Street Mill in 1933 (read more about arrastras on page 61). Bill moved the mill to the current Wall Street Mill site a couple of years later. He periodically milled his ore there and performed custom work for other mines in the area up to 1943.

Worth Bagley, a former deputy sheriff from Los Angeles, acquired property along the road to the Wall Street Mill in 1936. He immediately started butting heads with Bill Keys over water rights and use of the pre-existing road through his property to Wall Street Mill.

Upon Joshua Tree's designation as a national monument in 1936, it completely encircled Keys Desert Queen Ranch. With this came new problems for Bill Keys and other cattlemen. In 1937, area ranchers and cattlemen within the new monument were told they could no longer run their cattle at large without permission from the NPS.

Bill Keys had a difficult relationship with the NPS because of the new regulations limiting his cattle grazing, opening his water holes to the public, and restricting his homesteading and mining activities. Bill lived in the area for 27 years and resented the government regulations.

In May of 1941, President Roosevelt proclaimed an unlimited national emergency asking loyal citizens to step up productions for defense. Bill Keys applied for permission to Joshua Tree National Monument's Superintendent, James E. Cole (the monument's first Superintendent) to graze cattle on the public lands within the monument with the intent to produce more beef for national needs.

In 1942, Bill Keys met General George S. Patton. Patton established the Desert Training Center (DTC) in early 1942, and stationed troops throughout the Mojave Desert. The Mojave was a wasteland that had easy access to the railroad, and seemed to General Patton to be an excellent place to train troops during World War II. Camp Young and Camp Coxcomb were established next to Joshua Tree National Monument. Camp Young was the headquarters of the DTC, and was located near Shavers Summit (present-day Chiriaco Summit) just south of present-day Joshua Tree National Park.

After a year and a half of negotiations for grazing rights, Bill Keys was given permission to graze his cattle within the monument. After the end of WWII, all open range cattle grazing in Joshua Tree National Monument ceased.

On May 11, 1943, Bill Keys shot and killed Worth Bagley. Bill recounted that earlier in the day, he drove up the road to the Wall Street Mill in his 1928 Dodge. While he was at the mill, Bagley placed a sign on a stake in the middle of the road. After leaving the mill, Bill came upon something in the road blocking his path and he noticed it was the sign. As he drove closer to the sign, he could see what was written on it. It read; "KEYS, THIS IS MY LAST WARNING, STAY OFF MY PROPERTY." A short time later, he saw Bagley walking up the road towards him with a gun in his hand. As Bill ran back to his car, Bagley shot at him, but missed. Bill shot back in self-defense, killing Bagley. Keys turned himself in to authorities later in the day but they did not believe it was self-defense and charged him with manslaughter. At the age of 63, Bill was convicted and sentenced to ten years in San Quentin prison.

To help raise money for trial expenses and ranch bills, Frances sold 61 head of their cattle in 1943. When Frances put the word out that they were for sale, Kenny Paul, Joe Butler, and Harold Leinau from Palm Springs, CA agreed to buy the cattle together.

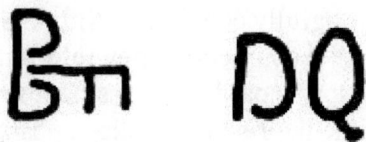

Cattle brands used by Bill and Frances

After graduating high school in 1939, Willis Keys lived in Alhambra, CA and began working near there. Virginia Keys graduated high school in 1941 and joined the Navy in 1942 soon after America's entry into WWII. While Bill was in prison, Frances lived in Alhambra and rented a house for her, Willis, Patricia, and Phyllis to live in. Patricia and Phyllis attended school there; Patricia graduated high school in 1945 and Phyllis graduated high school in 1948. Frances took a job in a defense plant and worked there until she returned to the ranch. Willis remained in Alhambra until he joined the Army in 1945.

During their time away, Frances' brother Aaron, who lived in Huntington Beach, CA, would occasionally stay at the ranch to keep things in working order. However, during their absence, the ranch house had been broken into and ranch property vandalized several times.

In 1948, Frances Keys wrote to Bill's friend, "The Court of Last Resort" attorney Erle Stanley Gardner (also author of the Perry Mason novels) and hired him to represent Bill. During an interview with Worth Bagley's widow (his ninth wife) on July 19, 1948, she said Bagley had intended to kill Bill Keys.

With Gardner's help, Bill accepted early release and immediate parole from San Quentin prison on October 25, 1948. The parole board came to the conclusion that Bill was innocent and wrongfully convicted. Although they could not overturn the court's conviction, they referred the case to the governor's advisory board for consideration of a pardon. Bill called his time in prison his college years, as he used the time to further his education. He was 69 when he left San Quentin.

Upon Bill's release from prison, he, Frances, and Phyllis moved back to the ranch to begin the necessary repairs caused by the vandalism and neglect during their absence. Bill picked up where he left off and undertook many improvements to the ranch, adding to the dams behind the ranch house, increasing his orchard and garden, raising the wall at Barker Dam, finishing the retaining wall behind the house, doing assessment work at his claims, and temporarily reopening the Wall Street Mill.

Sometime after his return home, Bill made and placed a stone monument at the spot where he killed Worth Bagley. It reads "Here is where Worth Bagley bit the dust at the hand of W.F. Keys May 11, 1943." The stone was later vandalized and eventually replaced with a to scale metal replica of the original monument.

Metal replica of the original monument

On July 12, 1956, the governor's advisory board ruled against the court's conviction of Bill Keys and he was granted an unconditional (full) pardon from Governor Goodwin Knight of California. The granting of the unconditional pardon fully restored Bill's civil rights forfeited upon his manslaughter conviction and restored his innocence as though he had never committed a crime.

17

By the mid-1950s, Keys Desert Queen Ranch and Joshua Tree National Monument were being visited by film-makers, Marines from a base in Twentynine Palms, Boy Scouts, and many others. "Wild Burro of the West," an episode of The Wonderful World of Disney, first aired on January 29, 1960. It was filmed in Joshua Tree National Monument and starred Bill Keys. Bill even got the chance to drive his Mack truck in the episode (read more about the Mack truck on page 56).

In the late 1950s, a group of wealthy equestrians from Palm Springs rode up to an area later named "Piano Rock" south of Barker Dam. They would have all their gear sent up ahead of them along with a chuck wagon where everything was prepared. This was a big event for them and was done annually. The group was led by Frank Bogert who would become mayor of Palm Springs.

On occasion, a piano was brought up and placed on a big flat rock just off of the present-day Barker Dam Trail and played for their entertainment. It had been rumored Bill Keys himself played the piano on Piano Rock on occasion but his son Willis dispelled this. In fact, at first Bill was angered about the loud piano and feared it would disturb the cattle. However, the piano music seemed to have an opposite effect and calmed them.

The Keys family knew the importance of working together as a team. With the closest doctor nearly 60 miles away, Bill and Frances kept medical journals at their ranch to treat any minor illness or injury they would encounter. They traded and negotiated with area homesteaders and businesses in nearby Twentynine Palms and later in the communities of Yucca Valley and Joshua Tree for everyday items such as salt, coffee, sugar, flour, cereal, and spices.

In addition to Erle Stanley Gardner, the Keys family hosted other well-known visitors such as prominent botanists Phillip Munz and Edmund Jaeger. During one of Jaeger's visits to the ranch, he identified a new desert flower, which he named "Keysia" (Glyptopleura setulosa) to honor the kindness the Keys showed to him and the many desert travelers who would visit.

Bill hoped to one day turn their ranch into a recreation resort. He wanted to create additional small lakes along the seasonal creek near the ranch house and provide camping and a picnic area for Boy Scouts and other youth groups, civic groups and clubs to use.

Frances Keys died on January 9, 1963 and was buried at the public cemetery in Twentynine Palms; she was 75. Bill Keys died on June 28, 1969, just three months short of his 90th birthday. He was buried in the family cemetery. Frances was moved from Twentynine Palms to the family cemetery.

Bill and Frances Keys; NPS photos

Excluding his time in prison, Bill Keys spent nearly 60 years of his life in and around his Desert Queen Ranch. He succeeded in the desert and through his resourcefulness, adapted to the ever-changing challenges he encountered each and every day. Bill had to be self-reliant and adamantly protected the needs and interests of his family. This attitude sometimes caused him to be at odds with people around him, especially when Joshua Tree National Monument was first formed. Even though Bill Keys could be difficult to work with at times, many of the surrounding homesteaders and miners considered Keys Desert Queen Ranch as the "center of their desert network" and thought of Bill and Frances Keys as their friends.

While the world outside the ranch changed dramatically, the Keys' way of life had remained remarkably constant. In 1994, the community of Twentynine Palms (through Action Council for 29 Palms, Inc.) commissioned a mural titled "Bill and Frances Keys" to commemorate the Keys family and to illustrate the impact they had on the area. Another mural was dedicated in 2013 titled "Keys' Desert Queen Ranch."

"Bill and Frances Keys"
by Dan Sawatzky and Peter Sawatzky;
courtesy of Action 29 Palms, Twentynine Palms, California, USA

"Keys' Desert Queen Ranch"
by Art Mortimer;
courtesy of Action 29 Palms, Twentynine Palms, California, USA

Desert Queen School

Frances first taught Willis then Virginia in the ranch house. Oran Booth had teaching experience and was hired in 1930 to teach the children. This would free up Frances to do other things that needed to be done around the ranch. Oran taught out of a temporary tent cabin in the beginning. At first, only Willis, Virginia and soon Ellsworth were taught there, but then other children from local homestead sites and mines started to attend the school. Oran worked in exchange for room and board.

Bill Keys converted the tent cabin into the first ranch schoolhouse not far from the ranch house in 1932 but they quickly outgrew it. He then moved school operations to the north house by the middle dam for a while. Lela Carlson (Perkins) was hired in 1933 to be their new teacher. Bill paid her a small salary and provided her room and board. As Bill and Frances had more children and more local children started to attend the ranch school, Bill built the southern schoolhouse to accommodate the many children.

Ellsworth, Virginia, Willis, and Patricia; NPS photo

Due to the number of students attending the ranch school, the San Bernardino County School Superintendent declared Desert Queen School an emergency school and began to pay towards school supplies and the teachers' salary in 1935. Once they moved the school to the southern schoolhouse in 1936, the house by the middle dam is where the school teacher lived.

The Desert Queen School, however, only taught as far as the eighth grade. At that point, students had to leave and attend high school at another location. Willis was the first to leave the Desert Queen School and moved to the Ontario, CA area to attend Chaffey High School in 1935. He would return to the ranch for his summer and school breaks.

After Lela Carlson (Perkins) left, Miss Starr became the teacher in the fall of 1935. Mrs. Marsh and her husband began teaching in September 1936. Della Dudley and her husband Howard were the last to teach at the school; they were hired in 1937. The Desert Queen School closed in 1942 after the youngest Keys child (Phyllis) left to attend school away from the ranch.

The Dudley's and school children, including Phyllis Keys;
NPS photo

The Ranch and the NPS

After the death of Frances, Bill Keys offered to sell his ranch to the National Park Service (NPS). Unfortunately, due to funding problems the NPS did not have the money to act. Bill then sold his Desert Queen Ranch to Henry "Hank" Tubman from Los Angeles in October 1964, with the exception of the one-acre family cemetery. Bill had only one provision, that he was allowed to live at the ranch until his death. Tubman agreed and started to make plans to build a dude ranch and resort there.

Not securing the necessary permits and with his financial backing fading away, Tubman abandoned his plans and began negotiations with the park service to sell the ranch to them. On October 28, 1966, Tubman traded Keys Desert Queen Ranch, all 879 acres, to the NPS for land in San Diego, CA. The land Tubman received in trade is the land where Qualcomm Stadium is located.

A photo of Bill Keys in his later years
in front of his ranch house; NPS photo

At one point, a team of historical specialists visited the ranch to decide its long-term fate. They recommended that the buildings be removed or allowed to disintegrate. This supported the monument's own leaders, who proposed a policy of "benign neglect" (noninterference). At the time, the most controversial site for preservation and interpretation at Joshua Tree National Monument was Keys Desert Queen Ranch.

After acquiring Keys Desert Queen Ranch, the National Park Service failed to provide funds to protect the ranch. However, in 1969 the NPS gave permission to Warner Brothers Pictures to build a replica of the Yuma Territorial Prison for the film "There Was A Crooked Man." The site was located 3 miles east of the Old Dale Road junction on Black Eagle Mine Road. In 1970, Warner Brothers donated $15,000 to Joshua Tree National Monument and the money was used to buy outlying mining claims, ranch equipment, and other ranch property from the from Key's heirs in 1971. With the purchase, the Superintendent promised one of the Keys daughters that the NPS would protect the ranch and one-day offer tours for park visitors.

In 1973, the NPS headquarters in Washington, D.C., ordered every unit in the national park system to develop a site to commemorate the nation's bicentennial in 1976. Since Keys Desert Queen Ranch had the largest collection of historic structures in Joshua Tree National Monument, it was the only realistic option. JTNM officials chose Keys Desert Queen Ranch to be the monument's bicentennial celebration site.

The decision to preserve it, its designation as a Point of Historical Interest by San Bernardino County in 1974, and its addition to the National Register of Historic Places on October 30, 1975, made Keys Desert Queen Ranch the largest display of cultural artifacts within the monument.

The National Park Service began giving guided tours of the Desert Queen Ranch in 1976 to commemorate the nation's bicentennial. The ranch is more commonly known today as Keys Ranch. Tours are seasonal and are typically held from October to May. They are generally not available during the hot summer months.

Key
1. Ranch House
2. Work Shed
3. Barn
4. Stamp Mill
5. School Teachers' House and Early School House
6. Concrete Dam
7. Lake
8. Supply Yard
9. Windmill
10. Orchard

Courtesy of the NPS; drawn by Reino Clark

To preserve its historic character, admission to the ranch is restricted to guided walking tours. Sadly, theft and vandalism have occurred at the ranch in the past as well as other locations within the park. Seasonal caretakers (park volunteers) live at the ranch to help keep an eye on it. They provide their own RV to live in while the park provides them with potable water and a sewage connection. There is no electricity throughout most of the park, including the ranch. Caretakers must have their own solar/battery system and generator to provide any electricity they may need.

Ranch tours are a half-mile in length and last about 90 minutes. Reservations are required in advance and the tour size is limited. Please note: tours may be canceled due to inclement weather and/or poor road conditions.

Sturdy walking shoes, drinking water, sunscreen, and a hat are highly recommended. Dress in layers to be prepared for changing weather conditions. Smoking and eating are not allowed during the tour. Camcorders and cameras are permitted but camera tripods and monopods are not. Dogs and pets are not permitted on this tour and cannot be left behind in the visitor's vehicle. Please arrive at the locked ranch gate at least 15 minutes prior to your tour.

Private tours of the ranch may be arranged by contacting park staff. You can inquire about special tours for photographers and other artists.

NO ONE is allowed on ranch property without being escorted by a park ranger or authorized park staff.

Keys Desert Queen Ranch Reservations:

For the tour schedule and how to reserve your tickets, visit the Joshua Tree National Park website, https://www.nps.gov/jotr

Backdrop along the tour

Keys Desert Queen Ranch Virtual Tour:

Whether or not you are able to attend the ranger-guided Keys Desert Queen Ranch tour in person, you can currently visit virtually with this three-part series that tells the story of what drew Bill Keys to this area, how he and Frances raised their family, and how they made a life in this harsh desert environment.

Visit the below website and click on the link under videos. https://www.nps.gov/jotr/learn/photosmultimedia/

The Ranch Tour

Your tour will begin at the locked gate outside of Keys Desert Queen Ranch. Visitors with reservations are asked to park outside the gate (not blocking it) and wait for the ranger to arrive to let them in.

Once the ranger has everyone accounted for, he/she will open the gate and drive forward, having everyone follow them. The ranger then stops their vehicle and walks back to close and lock the gate. Everyone then drives to the ranch visitor parking lot next to the ranches last-used schoolhouse.

The walking tour takes you along the road to the ranch by a wash crossing where you will find a site once used by American Indians long ago. There was once a spring nearby but it and most of the springs within present-day Joshua Tree National Park have long since dried up. Today during and after heavy rains or melting snow, the water can flow very fast along this wash, leaving pools of water. Near here is a small cave site where one could get shelter from the heat of the sun or the rain from a storm.

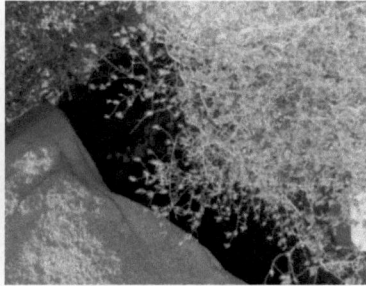

There is also an old bowl-like mortar created by American Indians that was hollowed into the rock and used to grind seeds, nuts and other bits of food into meal for hundreds of years. Pinyon Pine that produces pine nuts and Scrub Oak that produces acorns for use as a food source are nearby. The Serrano and Cahuilla Indians are believed to have inhabited this area as early as the 1500s to the 1800s. This is the only remaining visible evidence of the first inhabitants at the ranch site.

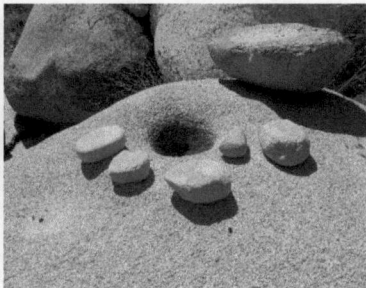

There are not many good wood sources in the desert and people had to find ingenious ways to make do with what they had. At the beginning of the ranch yard is one end of an old fence constructed of Joshua tree trunks. Joshua tree logs and trunks were used for various purposes in the early years. A Joshua tree log fence was also constructed in front of the ranch house.

In the late 1880s, the McHaney brothers established what came to be known as the "McHaney Camp." They built two adobe cabins at their camp. In 1894, the McHaney brothers built an adobe barn at the camp, just west of the adobe cabins. In about 1914, Bill Keys tore down the adobe cabins in order to clear the land, so he could extend the orchard southward. The original barn had two wings (lean-to's) used for animals, the main barn was for hay, feed, grain and chickens.

1950s aerial photo of Keys Desert Queen Ranch showing the old Adobe Barn; NPS photo

Photo of the old Adobe Barn with Bill Keys; NPS photo

The adobe barn started to fall apart around the 1930s. Bill later removed it in the 1950s. Not much of anything is left of the old barn today. There are a number of adobe brick molds scattered about.

The site where the adobe barn once stood

Bricks made from adobe are usually made by pressing the earth clay and organic material mixture into an open wood frame and left to dry and harden in the sun. This portable cement and adobe mixer was used to make the material needed to create the adobe brick used for building construction. The mixer was manufactured by the J. H. Day Co. of Cincinnati, OH, who began operations in the 1880s.

Wood forms were used to pour the adobe mixture into and were allowed to set before removing them for use.

The large open-top adobe hopper was erected in the 1950s. This is where Bill Keys would mix up his adobe brick mixture in large batches and then pour it into wood molds. It is the wooden structure located next to the machine shop.

Next to the large adobe hopper is what appears to be a well. However, this is a pit about 15 to 20 feet deep where Bill Keys dug clay to put in the hopper to make adobe brick.

The elevated water tank located next to the clay pit and adobe hopper was also erected in the 1950s. It received its water supply from the well at the windmill nearby. This water tower became the primary source for watering the orchard and garden, and supplying water to the ranch house.

The machine shop was built by Bill Keys in the 1930s when the adobe barn started to fall apart. It is located where the two original adobe cabins once stood. The shop is made of recycled material Bill would gather from abandoned claims and other mining sites, such as old metal water tanks that have been flattened out, wood flooring, and scavenged lumber he found throughout the desert. Inside the shop are all kinds of tools, supplies, used parts, bits and pieces of just about everything.

The old White Motor Company military surplus armored truck had been purchased by a man in Joshua Tree who converted it to haul a heavy drilling rig. With the help of his dad, Willis purchased the truck in 1953 and they put the current bed on it. He took off the rear box and adapted the truck for use around the ranch. The truck would go just about anywhere and they used to haul the heavier items.

In the late 1880s, the McHaney brothers dug this well to supply water for their adobe cabins. A windlass was first used to bring the water up (a windlass is a type of winch used to lower buckets into and hoist them up from wells). Sometime in the 1910s, Bill cleaned out the well and dug it deeper. Over the years, they had to continue to dig down even deeper to get to the water. He would also dig tunnels to go around the large rocks.

Bill Keys later added the windmill to the well

In 1936, Bill and Frances' ten-year old son Ellsworth was cranking the windlass to pull up a bucket of water. The metal handle either slipped out of his hands or the brake disengaged when he thought it was latched, and the metal handle struck him on the head. There were no doctors or hospitals nearby so Bill and Frances did what they could for Ellsworth. He never fully recovered from the injury and died the next year at age 11. Bill Keys installed a handpump shortly thereafter to make the job safer. The current windmill was later installed to do the work of the handpump. A gasoline engine was later used to pump the water.

 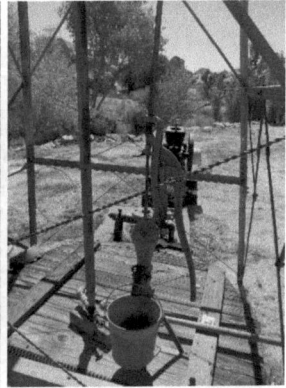

Windlass   Hand pump

Sometime in the late 1890s, the McHaney brothers dug out a well in the area of the current-day orchard. Bill first planted fruit trees there after he built his cabin and later, he and Frances planted several more. Bill used an auger to drill holes and then put 3 or 4 sticks of dynamite down them to blow a hole large enough to plant the trees. This would loosen the ground enough for trees to take root and grow.

In the early 1990s, various fruit trees were replanted in the orchard by the NPS based on a map Willis and others drew. However, many of the trees died in the years that followed.

Later, Bill and Frances expanded the family gardens. Fruits and vegetables from the garden and orchard were canned in amounts to provide for the whole family with food for the entire winter. Bill fertilized it with manure from horses, cattle, and mules.

They grew all types of vegetables and fruits in the garden, including corn, string beans, tomatoes, berries, and melons. The orchard had several kinds of apples, pears, apricots, peaches, crab apples, pears, and plums. At one time they had a large almond tree to provide shade for picnics.

Planted 1918 by B. Keys

The original water well in the center of the orchard eventually ran dry. Bill did not immediately cover the well and one day while plowing the field with a team of mules, one of them fell into the well. Luckily, Bill was able to get the mule out and he then covered the well. Bill ran water pipes throughout the orchard and garden, placing various water faucets with water supplied from the dam and the nearby water tower he erected in the 1950s.

During the summer months, it could rain hard for an hour or more causing the lake to fill up and the water to come over the dam. There were times the overflow was several feet high, endangering the orchard and house. Around 1940, Bill began to build a retaining wall along the wash to protect the orchard and house. He then began to build the wall by the house; however, work stopped on both projects while he served his time in prison.

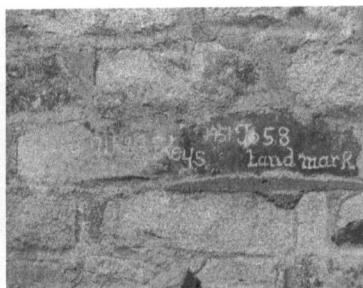

Bill made his own blocks by hand, using a hand crank drill, a hammer, wedges, and a chisel. He drilled holes every 3 to 4 inches in a straight line where he wanted to break the rock. Bill would then hammer steel wedges along the line to eventually break the rock apart, creating blocks. He used a crane boom with a tackle system and a heavy-duty tong to lift the heavy blocks into place to construct the wall. Bill resumed construction on the wall next to the house in 1951 and completed the work in 1958.

With the help of his friend Raymond "Ray" T. Bolster (an exceptional stonemason), Bill Keys began construction on an impressive chimney where he lived in 1913 at the Desert Queen Mill site. Bill then began to build a permanent cabin at the chimney. The original cabin had one long room with a porch and a room upstairs. The main floor of the cabin originally had a living/sleeping area at the fireplace and a kitchen at the other end. Once Bill acquired ownership of the Desert Queen Mill site, he immediately filed a homestead claim on the property in 1917. The chimney and fireplace were reportedly completed by this time.

Around 1919, Bill brought over an old cabin from the Desert Queen Mine and repurposed it into a new but small kitchen for their ranch house. The house grew as needed over the years. He soon added a bedroom onto the house for Frances. Bill enclosed part of the porch to the rear of the house in the mid-1920s, creating a little bedroom for the kids to sleep in. In the late 1920s, he added a larger bedroom for the kids, converting the first smaller one into a storage room. In the 1950s, Bill placed a modified 55-gallon drum on the top of the chimney to stop the north winds from blowing down it, forcing smoke into the house.

Frances' mother (Lena Lawton) would often visit; arriving in the spring and staying throughout the summer. She helped Frances with the canning and kept busy sewing patchwork quilts and sun bonnets. The room upstairs was where Lena stayed while visiting. When Lena was not there; Frances' brothers, family friends and visitors would stay in the upstairs room. That room would get very cold in the winter so Bill cut a small hole in the ceiling above the fireplace and built a trap door to allow heat to rise into the upstairs room.

In 1934, Bill acquired another cabin from the Roach Mine at nearby Gold Park Mining District to be used as a new kitchen. He removed the old smaller kitchen and attached the new larger one to the house (today's kitchen). Bill would eventually install a wood stove in the new kitchen. He also installed a desert cooler which reached through one of the windows to the outside. This cooler was a screened-in cabinet extending to the outside of the house (a bay window). The cabinet had a water pan on top with burlap sacks fastened down inside of the pan and the sacks were draped down over the exterior screen. In this method, the burlap sacks would siphon the water from the pan on top, keeping the sacks wet all the time. When the breeze blew through, it kept things cool. This is where they kept food such as milk and butter (see a photo of this window on page 82).

Bill would later acquire a propane refrigerator from one of General George Patton's nearby Desert Training Center camps. The camp had been abandoned and Bill filed a claim on the land in the mid-1940s and brought the refrigerator home.

Sometime in the mid to late 1930s, Bill acquired a bathroom from the El Dorado Mine in the nearby Pinyon Mining District and moved it to the ranch. Before this, they took sponge baths in front of the fireplace. For years, the new bathroom was set up in the west yard where they took hot showers. It wasn't until the 1950s when Bill finally attached the bathroom to the back of the ranch house and built a water heater for it.

To provide light within the house, they first used kerosene lamps. Sometime in the early 1940s Bill installed a generator behind the rocks on the north side of the house (to shield the noise to the house). This provided electricity for the house when needed. In the late 1940s, Bill moved the generator to the barn for protection from the weather.

Bill suffered from back trouble which gave him a lot of problems. Behind the house is a traction bench he constructed. When Bill's back went out, he would lie down on his back raising his arms above his head and had his kids attach the rope to his feet, cranked the winch and pulled his spine into alignment. He would lie there for about 30 minutes to an hour to get some relief.

The well located near the southwest corner of the ranch house was dug by Bill Keys right around the time the cabin was first built. This was the water source for most of their household needs. In 1944, Frances' brother Aaron took the casing out of this well and dug it out. He then bricked it up, added the arch frame above and attached a bucket and rope used to pull the water up. The Arundo donax (tall perennial cane) around the well was regularly watered by Frances with dirty dishwater.

Frances; NPS photo

45

In the early 1940s, Bill started to build the stone walls of the cabin next to the ranch house but it was not until 1951 when it was completed. It was used as a store for groceries and curios Frances would have extra to sell to local families and monument visitors. She even had a collection of unique items inside, which she called her museum collection. This building is more commonly known today as the "storehouse and museum."

Over a several year period, Frances collected a large amount of colored glass and bottles from old mining sites as she traveled around the area. Her collection grew so large, Bill built tables in front of the house so she could keep them in the sun to help with their color changing.

About every 2 weeks was wash day. The family used a gas powered 1929 Model 30 Maytag wringer-washer to do their laundry. They would build a fire under the wash tub to heat the water, put warm water into the washing machine and put the clothes in. They would then take them out, run them through the ringer and hang them on the clothes line to dry.

One day in late 1948, a doctor stopped by the ranch and wanted to buy a mining claim from Bill Keys. Bill admired the Willys Jeep the doctor was driving and offered to trade a mining claim for the Jeep. After the deal was struck the Jeep became Bill's favorite vehicle. It is one quarter ton, four-wheel drive and could go just about any place he would ever want to go. Originally, the Jeep had a canvas top which wore out regularly. In 1956, Willis took the Jeep down to Joshua Tree where he cut up an old Ford Model A, fitting its roof as a hard top for the Jeep. The Jeep legend began in November 1940, in the early days of World War II, a year before the United States entered the war. Willys Overland Motors, Inc./Jeep began in Toledo, OH.

Bill purchased the old Fordson Tractor from Phil Sullivan of Twentynine Palms. At first, Bill used this tractor to plough the orchard and garden area. He later converted it to be used in conjunction with the wood cutter. This came in real handy to cut up firewood. Fordson was a brand name of general-purpose tractors that were mass-produced starting in 1917 by Henry Ford & Sons!

Every ranch needed chickens to provide eggs for meals and the chickens themselves for meat. Bill Keys had a more unusual chicken coop than most people.

His came complete with the body of an old car! This is more commonly known today as the "chicken coupe."

Wagons were a common use in the early days on the ranch. They hauled a lot more than just ore. They were used for a trip to town to buy supplies, moving equipment from one place to another, or just taking the kids somewhere. The middle, larger wagon was manufactured by the Studebaker Company before they began making cars. Henry and Clement Studebaker set up a blacksmith shop in South Bend, IN in 1852, and soon started making wagons. The wagons were later replaced with motorized vehicles.

Whether you had a ranch, a mill site, a mine, or just a small cabin; you needed someplace to do your business. Keys Desert Queen Ranch was no different.

A story has been passed down over the years telling that when young, the Keys kids wanted to dig their own mine to find gold. Bill thought this was a great idea and showed them just where to dig. After digging down several feet and finding no gold or treasure, they lost interest. Bill took this opportunity to re-locate the "outhouse" to a new spot.

The Sears, Roebuck and Company catalog back in the day might have been kept in the outhouse, but was not necessarily used for reading!

During the 1959 filming and subsequent release in 1960 of "Wild Burro of the West," and "Chico, the Misunderstood Coyote," in 1961 (TV episodes of Walt Disney), Disney used this building to store equipment for filming and to possibly process their film on-site. The building is more commonly known today as the "Disney darkroom."

These two old cyanide vats were converted into a "tack room." Cyanide was used to separate the gold from the ore and could be very dangerous. Bill Keys had a knack of repurposing things, converting these vats for a more practical use of the day. He stacked one vat on top of another, connecting them and added a door on the side so the tack would be easy to access and kept out of the harsh weather.

When Bill filed on abandoned claims, he would repurpose everything he could, and this included the cabins. He would disassemble the cabins, bring them to where he wanted them, and reassemble them. This is one of the many cabins Bill would acquire and put into good use. This small cabin was assembled here in 1937-1938 and used as a "guest house" over the years. It was also used as a cabin people could rent if they were in the area for an extended stay.

Of the many things Bill Keys would collect and use was farming equipment. They would use them on the fields to grow hay and alfalfa as well as corn and other crops. When Bill no longer had use for the equipment, he had them out on display for anyone to purchase or trade for.

To help process the ore retrieved from mines, a crusher was sometimes used. A crusher is a machine designed to reduce large rocks into smaller rocks, gravel, or rock dust. There were various types of crushers in the industry. Below are just two types commonly used in this area.

Frances held school sessions for Willis and Virginia in the ranch house at first. Starting in 1930, Oran Booth was the first school teacher. This is a building once used as the small Desert Queen School and was built in 1932 by Bill Keys. It is located near the guest house. Oran taught the Keys children as well as children from other families in the area. After school operations were moved to the new schoolhouse by the lake, it was used for storage. Willis later used this cabin as his bedroom when he returned home from high school.

On the grounds, you will see several junked cars scattered all over. Some were bought and used by Bill Keys, some by Willis, and others Bill collected after they were abandoned and left behind. Whether they ran or not, he could always find use for the parts from these vehicles. Bill could also use the engines to run various machinery. He even made his own vehicles by welding together parts from different cars and trucks. In the 1940 Pioneer May Day parade in Twentynine Palms, Bill drove a vehicle he created by crossing an automobile with an Iowa farm wagon!

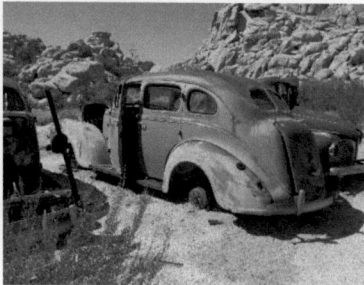

Bill Keys acquired this 1922 Mack truck in late 1948. The truck was believed to have belonged to the County of San Bernardino (one account lists it as once belonging to the City of San Bernardino) who abandoned it in the area. Finding the truck, Bill Keys brought it to the ranch. As far as Bill was concerned, they no longer wanted it and he did (finders, keepers). Bill Keys played the role of a prospector in the 1960 Disney film, "Wild Burros of the West" and drove the Mack truck in it. Mack Trucks was founded in 1900 by Jack and Gus Mack in Brooklyn, NY, and was originally known as the Mack Brothers Company.

As the Mack truck is part of the Keys Desert Queen Ranch tour, it had been parked in the same spot for many years and not moved until October 2005. One day, when a ranger arrived to give a tour, he noticed the Mack truck was not parked in its normal spot. At first, it was a great mystery how this may have occurred.

During one of Willis' many visits to the ranch, he told one of the rangers he bet the Mack truck could still run. So, she told him to give it a try and he did. Seeing what parts he needed, Willis returned the next day, fixed the truck and gave it a drive around the ranch. I would have loved to see the look on the face of the other ranger when he arrived the next day to give his tour.

The 1912 Traffic truck was used to haul gold ore and was acquired by Bill around 1940 from the Gold Coin Mine in the Pinyon Mining District. After he drove it to the ranch, he stripped it down, even removing the old 4-cylinder engine. In the early 1950s, Willis added the framework to the truck to help separate sand and gravel for making concrete. He planned to start a cement business but he would never finish this project.

In the beginning, the family mail box was located 36 miles away next to present-day Interstate 10 and State Route 62 (present-day Twentynine Palms Highway) near Whitewater, CA. There were a number of mail boxes located there for the residents surrounding the northern part of present-day Joshua Tree National Park. Since there were no established communities with post offices, this was the closest location where the US Mail would deliver. Twentynine Palms did not get their first post office until the 1920s, Yucca Valley, CA and Joshua Tree in the mid-1940s. When Joshua Tree opened their post office, Bill moved the family mail box near the intersection of present-day Twentynine Palms Highway and Park Blvd., in the community of Joshua Tree. This was closer to the ranch, as it was only 18 miles away. It remained there for years.

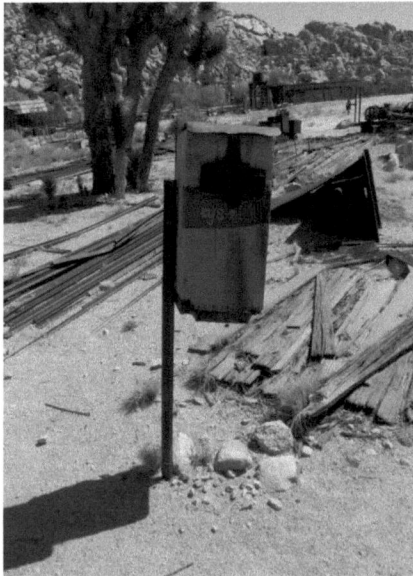

Zone Improvement Plan (ZIP) Codes were not used in the United States until their introduction nationwide on July 1, 1963. The US Postal Service used a cartoon character, which it called Mr. ZIP, to promote the use of the ZIP Code.

The ranch has piles of iron, metal pipes, various parts, and miscellaneous scrap. Bill bought out a junk yard once and moved everything to the ranch. If a part was needed at the ranch, mine or mill site, they would check their pile. If they did not have what they needed, it was easier to improvise it there rather than going to town to look for it. If they did not have what they needed, they made it.

Bill would collect unwanted old stoves and bring them back to the ranch. If Frances could use it, it was hers; otherwise they were available for sale or trade to anyone who needed it. Some of the models found here were made by Glenwood, Wedgewood, and Reliable gas stoves.

One item nearly every miner would need was a machine that brought fresh air to breathe into their mine. This machine did just that. A John Deere motor was connected to a belt driven Champion blower to provide air within the mine.

In mining, mercury was used to recover minute pieces of gold that was mixed in soil and sediments. A device similar to this could be used to melt off the mercury, leaving behind only the gold.

What mine would be complete without an ore car or two or three? Bill Keys had just about everything one would need to work their claim.

This arrastra was used by Bill Keys in conjunction with the one-stamp mill and other machines to crush the ore. It was built around 1932-1933. It replaced a smaller arrastra located where the old five-stamp mill was located on the ranch. An arrastra was a primitive method used by early miners to process gold ore. They were designed to extract gold which was locked inside rocks. The basic design generally used two large flat stones that were dragged around a circular pit made from flat stones. The drag stones were attached to a central pivot which allowed them to be dragged repeatedly over the ore that was placed in the arrastra. Arrastras were commonly used to train wild mules or horses. This got them used to the reins and harness. At first, they were typically powered by mules or horses, steam, or water. Later they were powered by a gasoline engine.

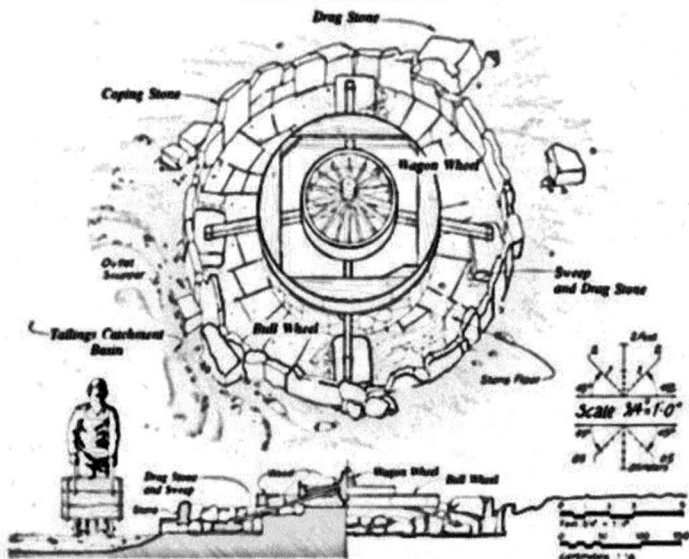

PINTO WYE ARRASTRA
JOSHUA TREE NATIONAL MONUMENT

SECTION

LOCATION MAP

Rendering of Pinto Wye Arrastra (similar to the arrastra located at Keys Desert Queen Ranch); by Ruth Connell

The one-stamp mill was brought to the ranch in 1924 by Bill Keys. He acquired it from a mill site in the Gold Park Mining District (near the north entrance of the park). It is one of the more efficient ways to crush ore to get the gold. Keys had his hand in some 30 mining claims throughout the area. Bill would also do custom mill work for other miners. Many of his claims were leased out to mining companies, providing a source of income for his family over the years.

A Stamp Mill is a mechanical ore crusher. They would haul it by wagon or truck to the mill site and assemble it there. The stamps were heavy metal weights that were lifted and dropped on the ore by a crankshaft. The crushed ore would then be further refined, usually by a mercury or cyanide process. These mills were noisy, heavy and somewhat awkward to operate. There were several ways to power a Stamp Mill. One way was a water wheel, another way was a steam engine. In later years, they were often powered by gasoline engines.

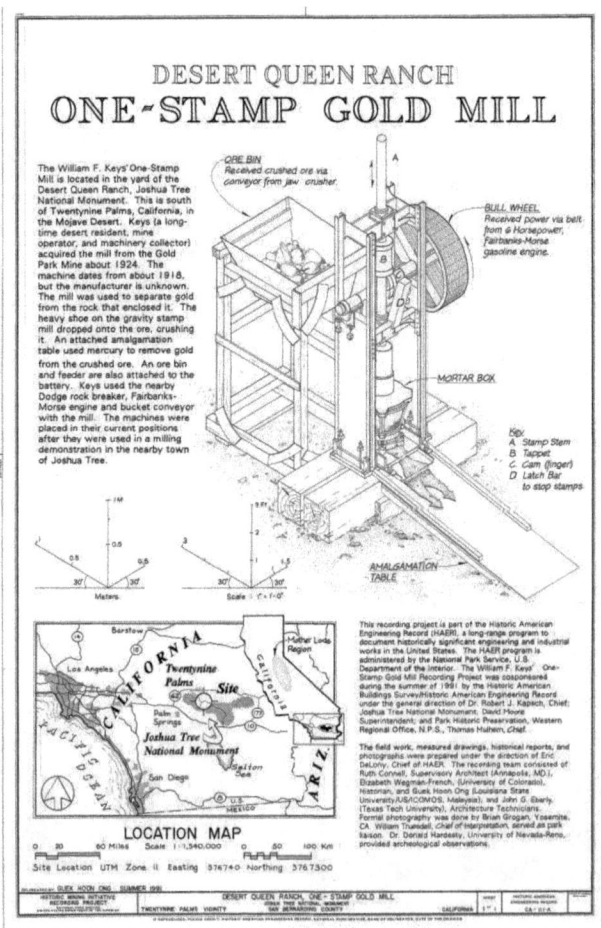

DESERT QUEEN RANCH
ONE-STAMP GOLD MILL

Bill McHaney moved to Keys Desert Queen Ranch in 1931 at the age of 72 and lived his final years in this cabin. Bill Keys rigged up an intercom system between the ranch house and McHaneys cabin. This allowed them to check up on him from time to time to make sure he was okay. They would call him to let him know they were walking over breakfast or dinner. McHaney enjoyed sharing his many stories with the Keys kids during this time. He lived there until his death in 1937. Over the years, the original cabin which Bill McHaney lived while staying at the ranch started to fall apart. The National Park Service later rebuilt the cabin as it appears today to help preserve its history.

"McHaney cabin"

Bill McHaney; NPS photo

This stick corral is original to the ranch, once connected to the adobe barn. Bill Keys built it out of willow poles and cable. Bill kept a small number of goats at the ranch at one time. He would also keep smaller animals in it.

The north house is located below the middle dam and was built by Bill Keys in 1919-1920 to serve as a guest house. Outgrowing the schoolhouse near the ranch house, school operations were moved here around 1933. By 1935, they outgrew this schoolhouse as well and moved to the new southern schoolhouse in 1936. The north house then served as the school teacher's cabin and is known today as the "lake cabin."

This cabin consists of a living room/bedroom area in the front, a screened in porch area to the side and a kitchen to the rear (the kitchen was added after it was no longer being used as a schoolhouse and then became the school teacher's house). Bill built the kitchen sink out of a boulder protruding out of the hillside. He built the kitchen wall around the rock. The lake cabin was stabilized and restored by the NPS in 1993.

This is an old Chilean Mill. It is believed to have been installed in 1916 by Bill Keys but used for only a short time. A Chilean Mill typically has two or more rotating wheels that would revolve over a pan filled with ore. The idea was that the wheels would break open the rocks with gold, so they could extract gold from more than one rock at a time. Bill dismantled the Chilean Mill in 1963.

The adobe building next to the Chilean Mill was started by the McHaney brothers, but not much else is known about this site. In the 1930s, Bill Keys built a fireplace and started to put up the adobe walls but never got around to putting on a roof. Consequently, the adobe bricks melted down over the years.

The McHaney brothers purchased and had installed a five-stamp mill from Baker Ironworks of Los Angeles at this site in 1895. Just parts of the foundation remain today. A water well was dug by the McHaneys at this site. This provided water for the steam engine which powered the stamp mill. The mill was later removed and sold by Bill Keys sometime after 1948.

An early arrastra built by Bill Keys during an unknown year was built next to the five-stamp mill. It was not used long as he built a larger one nearer the ranch house.

The southern schoolhouse was built in 1935-1936, and the last one used before the youngest Keys child left to attend school away from the ranch. It is located next to the current visitor parking lot at the ranch. The schoolhouse was heated with a tall heater Bill purchased from the Montgomery Ward catalog. The original schoolhouse consisted of just one room. In the early years, Frances needed a larger kitchen on the ranch house so Bill removed their small kitchen from the ranch house and dragged it over to this schoolhouse and connected them together, using it as a storage room. The school was closed in 1942.

From Cabin to Ranch House

Cabin floor plan circa 1914-1919

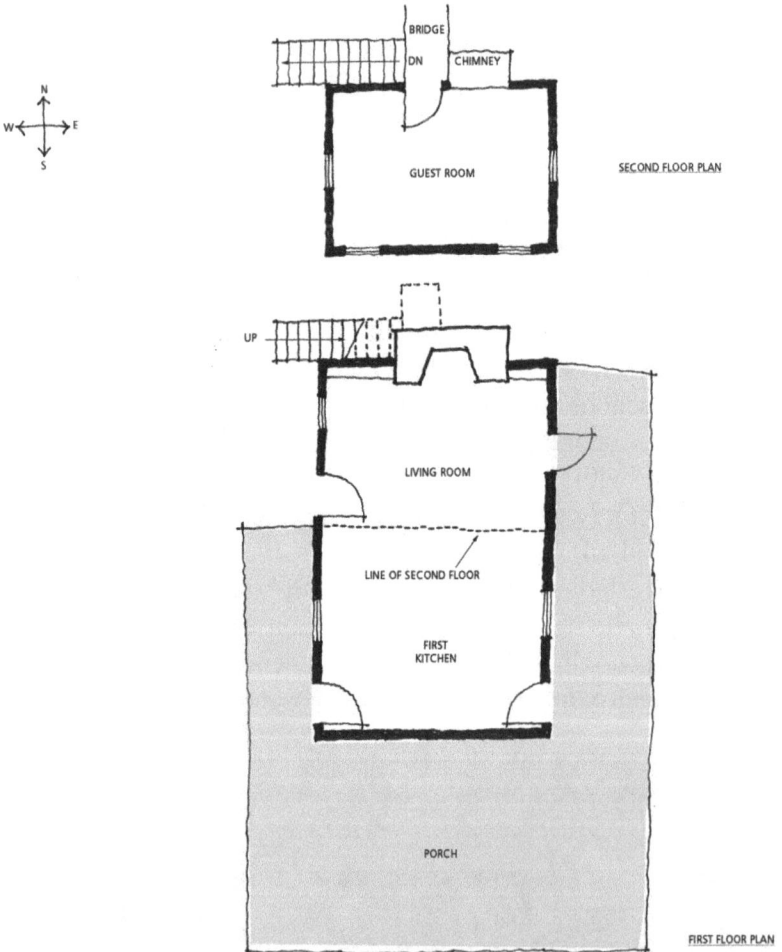

BRIDGE

DN | CHIMNEY

N
W — E
S

GUEST ROOM

SECOND FLOOR PLAN

UP

LIVING ROOM

LINE OF SECOND FLOOR

FIRST
KITCHEN

PORCH

FIRST FLOOR PLAN

The cabin in its original form.

The ranch cabin was first completed in 1914. Over the years, the cabin grew as the family grew, becoming the ranch house we see today. These NPS illustrations show the transformation from a cabin to a ranch house throughout the years.

Cabin floor plan circa 1919-1923

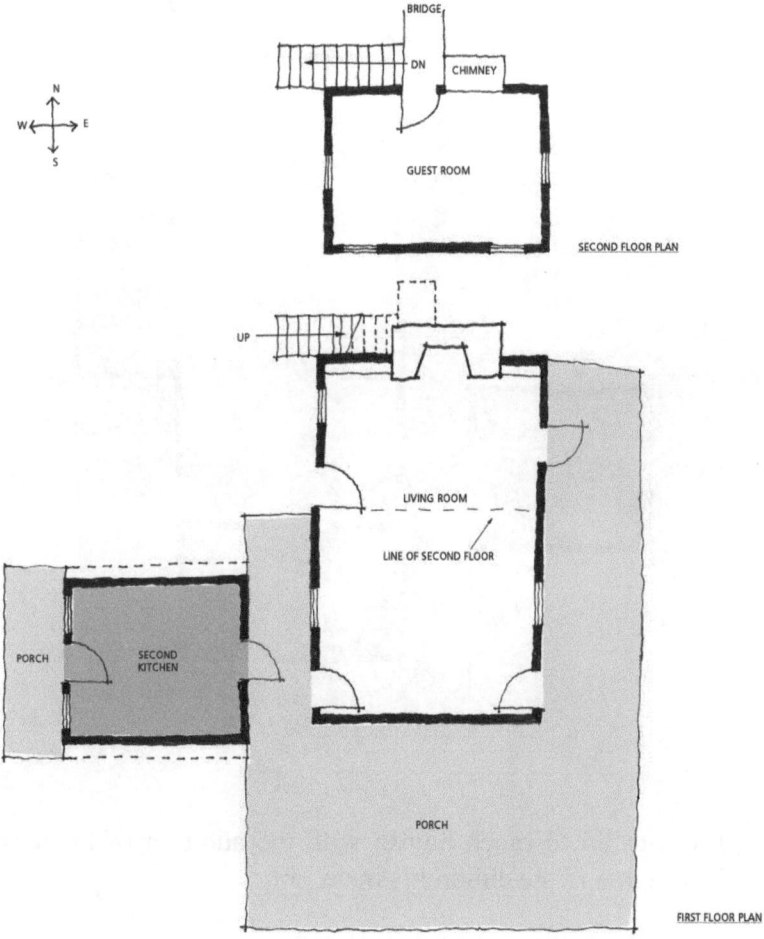

The cabin with the addition of the detached second kitchen.

Ranch house floor plan circa 1923-1928

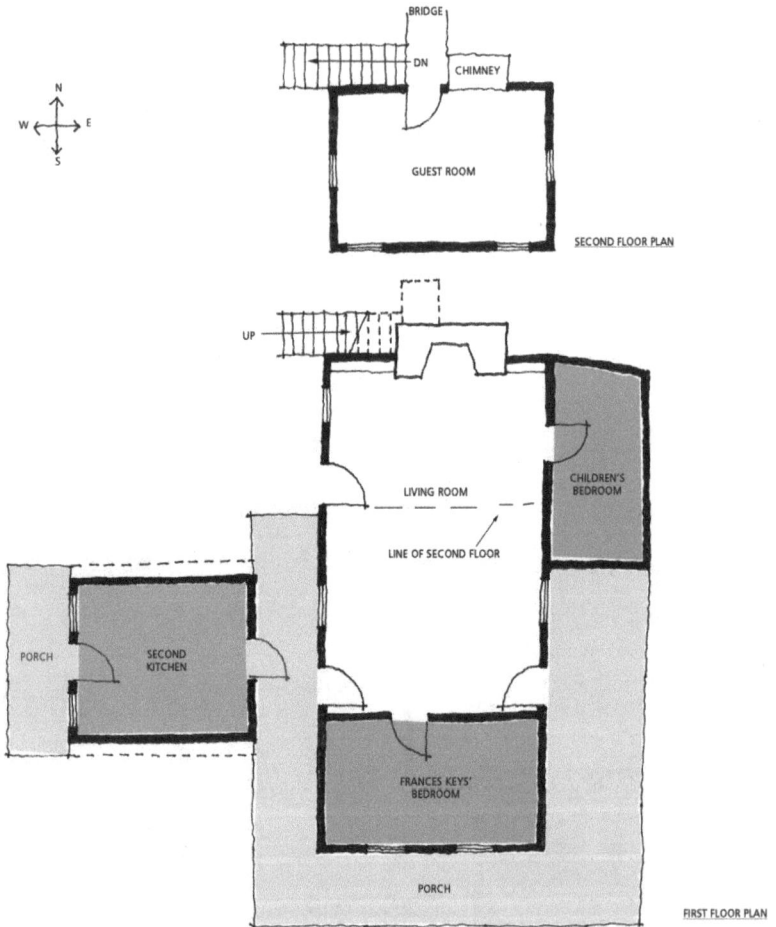

From cabin to ranch house; with the addition of Frances' bedroom and the children's bedroom.

Ranch house floor plan circa 1928-1934

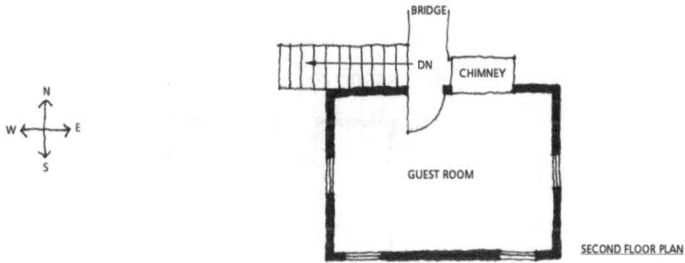

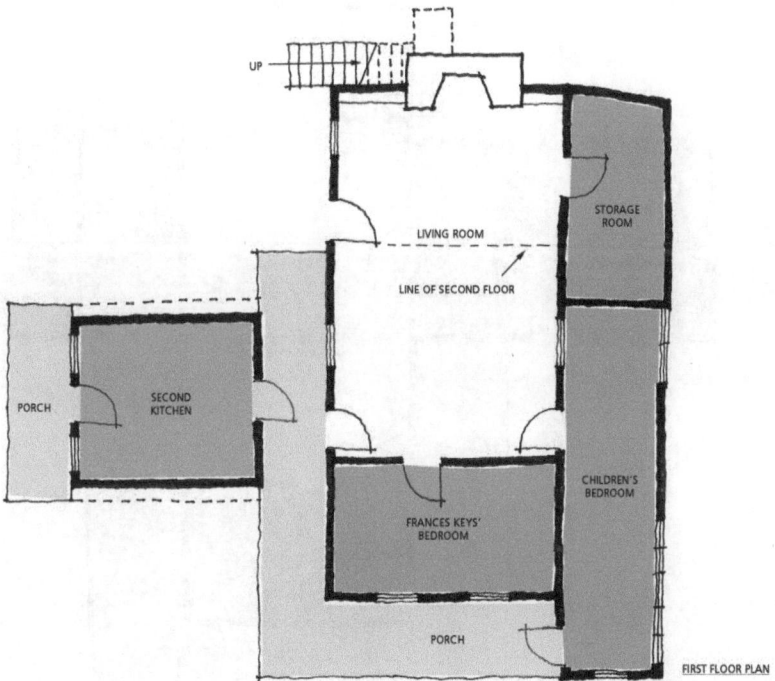

The ranch house; converting the children's bedroom into a storage room and adding a larger bedroom for the children.

Ranch house floor plan circa 1934-1965

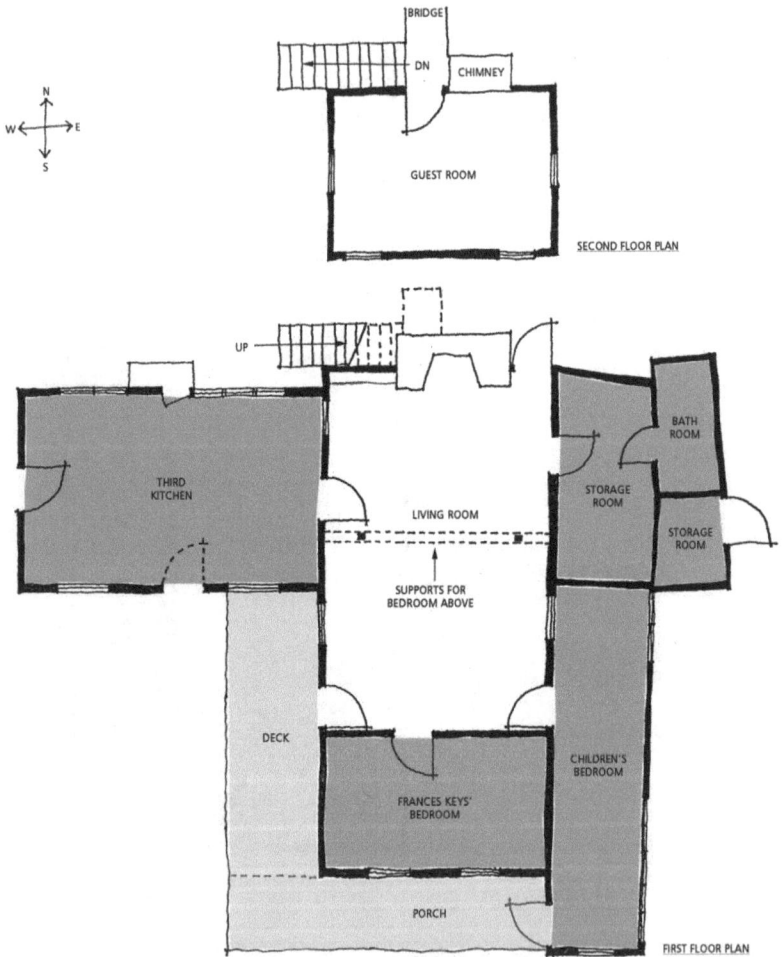

N
W←→E
S

BRIDGE
DN CHIMNEY

GUEST ROOM

SECOND FLOOR PLAN

UP

THIRD KITCHEN

LIVING ROOM

SUPPORTS FOR
BEDROOM ABOVE

BATH ROOM

STORAGE ROOM

STORAGE ROOM

DECK

FRANCES KEYS'
BEDROOM

CHILDREN'S
BEDROOM

PORCH

FIRST FLOOR PLAN

The ranch house with the addition of the new and larger third kitchen as well as the bathroom and an additional storage room.

Ranch house floor plan circa 1965-present

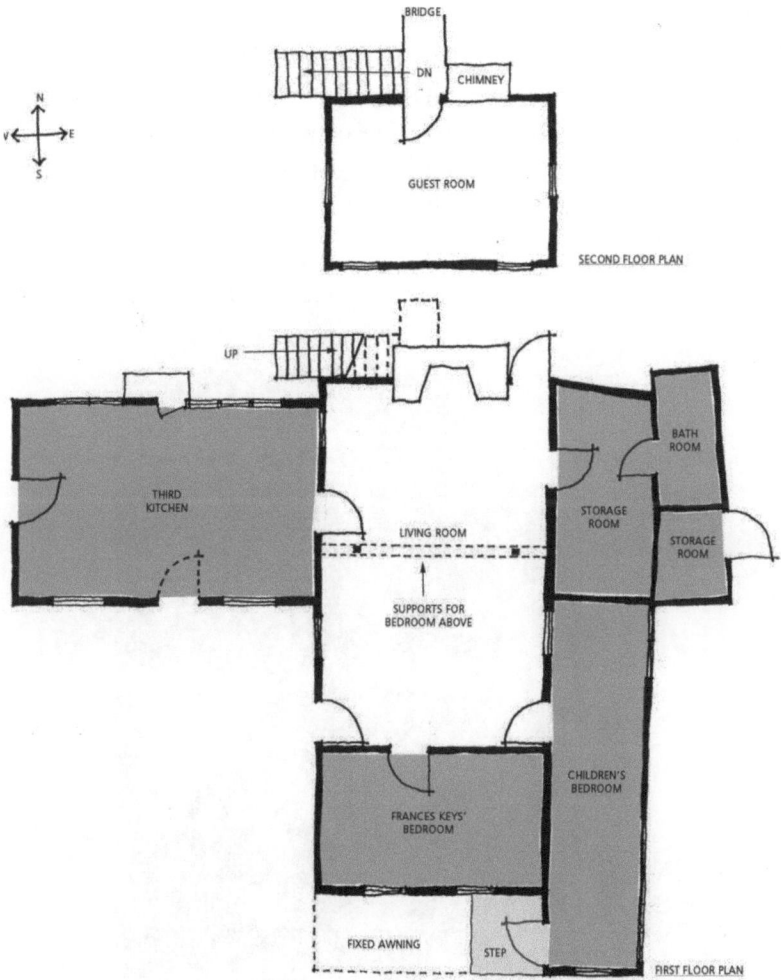

The ranch house; eliminating the deck and porch and attaching a fixed awning.

The Dams Protecting
the Ranch

The first dam Bill Keys built is the northern most dam (up above the outhouse for the lake cabin). He built this dam around 1914. A pipeline came from this dam to help provide water for the orchard next to the house in addition to the water tower next to the machine shop.

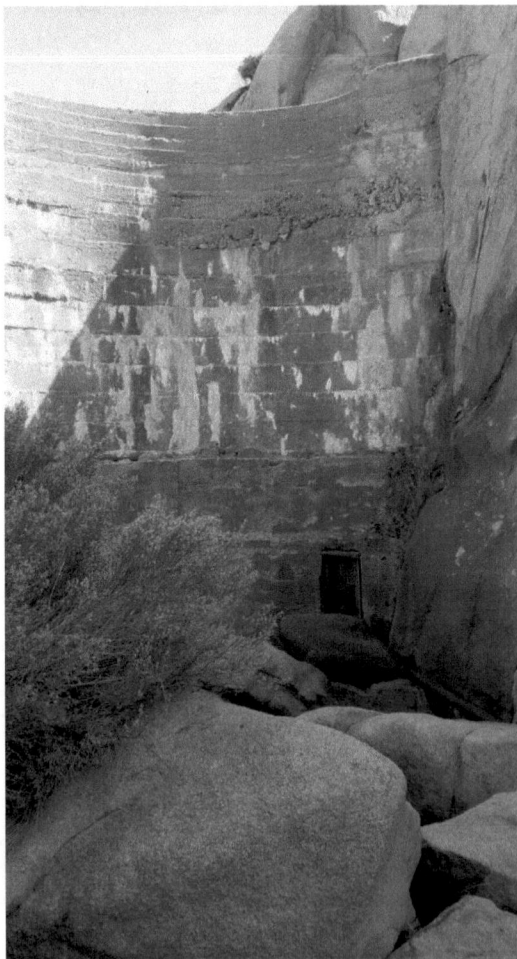

After a lake began to form up behind the northern dam, the water began to run out where the present-day south dam is located. Bill built a dirt levee in the area of the southern dam (above their house) to contain the water. In the early 1920s, Bill and Frances completed an earthen dam at this site but it later washed out and was replaced by a cement dam in the early 1930s (present-day southern dam). The water from this dam was used for crops, to water livestock and later for the stamp mill. Bill called it Keys Lake and stocked it with fish. Around 1934, after a long drought, the lake dried up and they lost all the fish. During the winter of 1948/1949, the lake froze over, about 2-feet thick. This enabled the children the opportunity to ice skate on their lake. They would make improvements on this dam up to the 1950s.

The third and final dam at the ranch is the one behind the lake cabin. Concerned about the lake overflowing, Bill built this dam around 1951 to protect the cabin.

NO ONE is allowed at or near any of the dams without being escorted by a park ranger or authorized park staff.

The Ranch under the Stars

Joshua Tree National Park was designated as the 10th International Dark Sky Park in the U.S. National Park system by the International Dark-Sky Association (IDA) in 2017. The Dark Sky designation is part of a growing movement across the nation and around the world that wants skies illuminated by stars. The park strives to be a refuge for those who want to experience a naturally dark night sky. Rangers often offer programs about the wonders of the night sky and our ongoing relationship with it. The following night-time photos were taken by local artist/photographer, Marjorie Trandem.

Keys Desert Queen Ranch takes on a whole new light under the night skies of Joshua Tree National Park.

On occasion, The Desert Institute offers "Night Sky Photography" classes; some of which have been held at Keys Desert Queen Ranch. The Desert Institute offers classes for adult learners in cultural history, natural science, survival skills, desert naturalist studies, women's programs, citizen science, and creative arts. The Desert Institute is sponsored by the Joshua Tree National Park Association, and operates with the full endorsement of the NPS. JTNPA is the parks "official" non-profit partner. To learn more about classes offered by The Desert Institute, go to www.joshuatree.org

To view more of Marjorie Trandems amazing photos, visit her website at: https://marjorietrandem.smugmug.com/

The Ranch in the Snow

      Keys Desert Queen Ranch is not only located within the Wonderland of Rocks, it can be a winter wonderland at times. Although snow in Joshua Tree National Park is not uncommon, usually only a dusting occurs and melts soon after the sun comes up. On occasion, the park gets a good snowfall that may last a day or two before completely melting. The photos below are from the December 26, 2019 storm that deposited several inches of snow in the park, including Keys Desert Queen Ranch. This snowpack lasted over a week!

The ranch in the snow photos are courtesy of the 2019/2020 seasonal ranch caretakers, James and Cheryl Kubow.

The 1976 Tour Guide

The cover page and map below are from the original ranch tour guide of 1976. The guide was written by Reino and Wendy Clark and contained 18 pages of information, photos, sketches, and a map of the tour of the ranch.

THE   15¢

DESERT

QUEEN

RANCH

By Reino and Wendy Clark

This is the story of an isolated, rock-bound canyon on the southern edge of the Mojave Desert. The trickle of water at its bottom has set it apart for thousands of years, making it special in a land of searing heat and dryness. From the first day of its discovery by wildlife taking advantage of its sandy pools, to the time when sunburned prospectors dipped their gold pans into the cool waters, the site has buzzed with activity. This desert alcove has meant life for untold numbers, and many generations of men and women have lingered here, all leaving their marks upon the land.

1776 U.S. BICENTENNIAL 1976

Produced in Cooperation
with the
NATIONAL PARK SERVICE
1975

JOSHUA TREE NATIONAL MONUMENT
74485 PALM VISTA DRIVE
TWENTYNINE PALMS, CALIFORNIA 92277

The Desert Queen Ranch

Trails and points of interest

Homesteads

Homesteads were made possible under the Homestead Act of 1862. The act was signed into law by President Abraham Lincoln on May 20, 1862. This act encouraged western migration by providing settlers 160 acres of public land. In exchange, homesteaders paid a small filing fee and were required to build an inhabitable dwelling and to live on the property for five years before receiving ownership of the land.

In the mid-1950s, Joshua Tree National Monument had become well established within the National Park system. Although homesteading was no longer allowed in the monument, small cabins began being built adjacent to and around the park. This was made possible under the Small Tract Act of 1938. In the late 1940s, the Southern California Desert was opened up for new 5-acre homesteads. One of the requirements was that the property to be improved with a building of 400 sq. feet of space minimum (a cabin). These smaller homesteads became known as "Jackrabbit Homesteads."

The Homestead Act was officially repealed in 1976 by the Federal Land Policy and Management Act. However, a ten-year extension allowed homesteading in Alaska until 1986. In all, the government allotted over 270 million acres of land in 30 states under the Homestead Act.

"Jackrabbit Homestead"; Crochetiere family photos

Mines and Mills

On average, mining claims were 20 acres each and mill sites of 5 acres each. Joshua Tree National Park contains an estimated 300 abandoned mine sites, each typically including a shaft, a tunnel, a small tailings pile (crushed rock dump), a can dump, and perhaps the outline of rocks where a miner once pitched a tent. Approximately 120 abandoned mine sites in Joshua Tree have a substantial opening and may represent a safety hazard. Twenty-one are old "mill sites" where gold was extracted from ore, leaving historic remains, but also potentially hazardous waste.

In 1996 a new technique for covering mineshafts was tried by the NPS. A plastic foam product called PUF (polyurethane foam), similar to the material used for home insulating, was injected into the opening of the mineshaft to provide a stabilizing plug. The plug was then covered with fill dirt to protect it from UV damage and a wooden replica of the shaft collar was constructed. This technique is called "puffing" the mine.

In addition to "puffing" the mine to close some of the shafts, the park service installed "gates" on other mines to create a safety barrier to people but still allow entry to colonies of bats that may wish to use the abandoned mine. There are no active mines or mill sites within Joshua Tree National Park today.

Present-day "gated" Desert Queen Mine

About the Author

Thomas Crochetiere works with the National Park Service at Joshua Tree National Park as an Interpretation/Visitor Service Representative. After retiring from a career in public service, he began working with the NPS in 2013. From the more than 302,000 eligible volunteers, Thomas was recognized for his contributions to the park service during the NPS National Volunteer Week in April 2019 and featured in an article titled "NPS Meet Our Volunteers: Tom Crochetiere." He is also a volunteer with the Desert Regional Tourism Agency at the California Welcome Center in Yucca Valley as a Welcome Ambassador. Thomas is a member of the Morongo Basin Historical Society and the Hi-Desert 4x4 Group of Yucca Valley.

Thomas is an avid traveler; having visited all 50 states, and is in the process of doing it all again. A devoted park visitor, he is passionate not only about Joshua Tree National Park but about all of our National Park units and enjoys sharing them with others.

Photo by Sandra Crochetiere

Notes